PRINCEWILL LAGANG

Relationship Finance: Managing Money as a Team

Contents

1

Introduction

In a world characterized by ever-evolving dynamics in personal and financial spheres, the significance of financial management in relationships cannot be overstated. As individuals embark on journeys of togetherness, whether through marriage, cohabitation, or partnership, the realm of finances intertwines deeply with their shared aspirations and goals. This chapter aims to underscore the pivotal role that financial management plays in the health and longevity of relationships, while also highlighting the numerous advantages that arise from approaching finances as a unified team.

1.1 The Intricacies of Financial Interdependence

At the heart of every relationship lies a complex web of interdependence, wherein emotional, social, and financial ties weave together to create a tapestry of shared experiences. Financial matters, often deemed as mundane or stressful, have a unique ability to shape the very core of these relationships. Whether it's planning for the future, handling day-to-day expenses, or navigating unexpected financial challenges, the manner in which couples manage their finances can significantly impact the stability and harmony of their partnership.

1.2 Beyond Dollars and Cents: The Emotional Weight

Financial decisions are rarely confined to the realm of numbers; they carry emotional weight that can either strengthen or strain a relationship. Disagreements over money can unearth underlying issues of trust, communication, and differing values. A failure to address these emotional aspects can lead to resentment, distance, and even separation. This chapter will delve into how open conversations about finances can serve as a means to not only manage money but also to foster emotional intimacy and understanding.

1.3 The Power of Unity: Approaching Finances as a Team

The old adage "two heads are better than one" rings particularly true when it comes to financial management in relationships. Collaborative efforts in handling finances can lead to a myriad of benefits, from shared financial goals that enhance mutual growth to a sense of collective responsibility that eases the burden of decision-making. This chapter will explore the advantages of jointly navigating financial waters, emphasizing how couples can leverage each other's strengths and perspectives to create a solid foundation for their financial journey.

1.4 Outline of the Book

As we embark on this exploration of financial management within relationships, subsequent chapters will delve into the practical aspects of effective financial communication, strategies for setting joint financial goals, methods to divide financial responsibilities equitably, and approaches to weathering financial storms as a united front. By delving into real-life stories, expert insights, and actionable advice, this book seeks to empower couples to not only manage their finances effectively but also to cultivate a deeper, more resilient connection.

In conclusion, the chapters that follow will shed light on the intricacies of financial management in relationships, offering guidance and perspectives to help couples navigate the challenges and opportunities that financial matters present. By embracing the principles of open communication, mutual respect, and collaborative decision-making, couples can forge a path towards financial stability, emotional intimacy, and enduring partnership.

2

Aligning Financial Goals

I n the journey of a partnership, shared financial goals serve as the compass that guides couples towards a future of harmony, security, and mutual growth. This chapter delves into the profound importance of aligning financial aspirations and provides strategies for setting and prioritizing these objectives collaboratively.

2.1 The Foundation of Shared Dreams

Every partnership is unique, a fusion of two individuals with distinct backgrounds, dreams, and ambitions. However, it's the harmonization of these individual aspirations into a collective vision that sets the stage for financial success. Shared financial goals lay the groundwork for unified efforts, enabling couples to embark on a joint financial journey with a clear purpose. This section underscores the role of these goals in fostering cooperation, mutual understanding, and a sense of direction.

2.2 The Process of Goal Setting

Setting financial goals is an art that requires a blend of foresight, realism, and aspiration. This section outlines a systematic approach to goal setting within relationships:

2.2.1 Open Dialogue: Effective communication is the cornerstone of goal setting. Partners must engage in open conversations to understand each other's financial aspirations, values, and concerns. These discussions provide insights into short-term and long-term objectives, forming the basis for goal alignment.

2.2.2 SMART Criteria: Utilizing the SMART (Specific, Measurable, Achievable, Relevant, Time-bound) criteria can transform vague desires into tangible targets. Couples can work together to refine their goals, ensuring they are realistic, quantifiable, and well-defined.

2.2.3 Prioritization: Partners often have a multitude of financial objectives, ranging from buying a home to saving for retirement. This section delves into techniques for prioritizing goals based on urgency, impact, and alignment with broader life plans.

2.3 Navigating Differences

Differing financial priorities are not uncommon, but they need not lead to conflict. Instead, these disparities can spark valuable conversations that uncover underlying values and priorities. This section explores strategies for finding common ground and devising compromises that honor both partners' aspirations.

2.4 Reaping the Benefits of Shared Financial Goals

Aligned financial goals not only provide clarity but also bestow couples with a range of advantages:

2.4.1 Unity and Mutual Support: Working towards shared objectives fosters a sense of unity and shared purpose. Partners can rely on each other for motivation and encouragement, forging a strong partnership built on common aspirations.

2.4.2 Enhanced Decision-Making: With a clear roadmap, couples can make informed financial decisions that directly contribute to their shared vision. This minimizes conflict arising from impulsive choices and ensures a consistent direction.

2.4.3 Resilience in Challenges: A joint financial journey is better equipped to weather unexpected challenges. The foundation of shared goals offers couples the resilience and determination needed to navigate financial hardships.

2.5 Cultivating Flexibility and Growth

While aligning goals is crucial, relationships evolve, and so should financial aspirations. This section emphasizes the importance of revisiting and adjusting goals periodically. Flexibility ensures that the financial path remains in harmony with changing circumstances and new opportunities.

2.6 Guided Exercises and Reflections

To facilitate the implementation of the concepts discussed, this chapter concludes with practical exercises and reflective prompts. These tools empower couples to engage in meaningful conversations, uncover shared dreams, and lay the groundwork for a unified financial future.

In the subsequent chapters, we'll explore how to put these aligned financial goals into practice, including effective methods of tracking progress, managing joint finances, and overcoming potential roadblocks. By embarking on this journey together, couples can harness the transformative power of shared financial aspirations, weaving their individual narratives into a collective tale of prosperity and fulfillment.

3

Understanding Money Mindsets

Money isn't just currency; it's laden with beliefs, emotions, and experiences that shape the way individuals perceive and interact with it. In a partnership, these individual money mindsets can significantly impact the dynamics of the relationship. This chapter delves into the intricacies of these mindsets, explores their influence on partnerships, and provides strategies to navigate divergent financial attitudes while seeking common ground.

3.1 Unraveling Money Mindsets

Behind every financial decision lies a complex tapestry of beliefs, often rooted in upbringing, culture, and personal experiences. This section emphasizes the need for partners to understand and acknowledge their own money mindsets before attempting to understand their significant other's. Exploring topics like saving, spending, investing, and risk tolerance can unveil deeply ingrained attitudes that influence financial behavior.

3.2 The Ripple Effect on Relationships

Understanding money mindsets becomes paramount as these beliefs don't exist in isolation. Instead, they cast a ripple effect that extends to the partnership as a whole. Disparities in money attitudes can lead to misunderstandings, conflict, and a sense of disconnect. Conversely, awareness and appreciation of these differences can create opportunities for growth, compromise, and enhanced communication.

3.3 Navigating Differences

Divergent money mindsets are natural, but they needn't be divisive. This section explores approaches to navigating these differences:

3.3.1 Active Listening: Partners must create safe spaces for honest conversations about their money beliefs. Active listening fosters empathy, allowing each individual to understand the origins and reasons behind the other's mindset.

3.3.2 Finding Common Ground: While differences may exist, there are often areas of alignment. Identifying shared values and goals can pave the way for cooperative financial decisions that resonate with both partners.

3.3.3 Compromise and Flexibility: Relationships thrive on compromise. This section delves into how partners can negotiate and find middle ground, accommodating each other's money preferences without disregarding their own.

3.4 Transformative Communication

Effective communication about money mindsets can lead to transformative outcomes:

3.4.1 Vulnerability and Authenticity: Sharing personal money stories, fears, and aspirations fosters vulnerability and authenticity. Partners can bond over shared experiences and lend support to each other's challenges.

3.4.2 Collaborative Decision-Making: Partners can harness their diverse money perspectives to make more informed decisions. A fusion of different attitudes often results in well-rounded choices that consider a broader spectrum of factors.

3.4.3 Emotional Intimacy: Conversations about money, when approached with empathy and respect, can lead to deeper emotional intimacy. Understanding each other's fears and desires builds trust and connection.

3.5 Integrating Money Mindsets

While each partner may retain their distinct money mindset, the journey towards a harmonious partnership involves integration:

3.5.1 Joint Vision: Creating a shared financial vision that accommodates both partners' money beliefs ensures that decisions align with overarching aspirations.

3.5.2 Ongoing Dialogue: Money mindsets can evolve over time. Regular conversations ensure that evolving beliefs are understood and integrated into the partnership's financial journey.

3.5.3 Professional Guidance: In cases where money mindsets lead to persistent disagreements, seeking the guidance of financial professionals or therapists can provide an unbiased perspective and strategies for resolution.

3.6 Guided Reflection and Action

To facilitate a deeper understanding of money mindsets and their impact, this chapter concludes with reflective exercises and action steps. These tools empower couples to engage in meaningful discussions, foster empathy, and lay the foundation for a partnership that acknowledges and respects each other's money beliefs.

In the forthcoming chapters, we will explore practical strategies for managing joint finances, making informed decisions, and overcoming challenges. By embracing the diversity of money mindsets and fostering an environment of openness, partnerships can evolve into powerful platforms for mutual growth and understanding.

4

Effective Communication

In the realm of relationships, the power of effective communication cannot be overstated. When it comes to financial matters, open and transparent dialogue forms the bedrock of a healthy partnership. This chapter delves into the pivotal role of communication in navigating money-related discussions and offers techniques for approaching these conversations constructively.

4.1 The Foundation of Financial Harmony

Financial communication is more than just talking about numbers; it's about understanding each other's perspectives, values, and concerns. Open communication is the gateway to resolving differences, aligning goals, and fostering emotional intimacy. This section underscores the significance of communication in laying the foundation for financial harmony.

4.2 Breaking Down Barriers

Financial conversations can be fraught with tension due to the taboo surrounding money. However, embracing the vulnerability of these discussions can lead to transformative outcomes:

4.2.1 Creating Safe Spaces: Partners must establish safe environments free from judgment or blame, where both individuals feel comfortable sharing their thoughts and feelings about money.

4.2.2 Removing Assumptions: Assumptions often fuel misunderstandings. Partners should actively seek clarification rather than assuming they understand the other person's perspective.

4.2.3 Embracing Empathy: Empathy is the cornerstone of effective communication. Partners should strive to understand each other's emotions and concerns before moving on to problem-solving.

4.3 Techniques for Constructive Conversations

Navigating financial conversations effectively involves employing communication techniques that foster understanding and resolution:

4.3.1 Active Listening: Attentive listening is a fundamental skill. Partners must truly listen, without interrupting, to comprehend each other's viewpoints before formulating responses.

4.3.2 "I" Statements: Framing statements with "I" instead of "you" minimizes blame and defensiveness. For example, saying "I feel concerned about our budget" is less confrontational than "You're spending too much."

4.3.3 Clarifying and Summarizing: After each partner speaks, the other should clarify and summarize to ensure that they've understood correctly. This prevents misinterpretations.

4.3.4 Asking Open-Ended Questions: Open-ended questions encourage more elaborate responses, facilitating deeper conversations. For instance, "How do you envision our financial future?" invites a more detailed response than "Do you want to save more?"

4.4 Timing and Environment

The when and where of financial conversations matter:

4.4.1 Choose the Right Time: Avoid discussing finances when emotions are running high or during other stressful situations. Instead, choose a time when both partners are calm and focused.

4.4.2 Neutral Settings: Opt for neutral settings that minimize distractions and interruptions. This fosters an environment conducive to focused and respectful conversation.

4.5 Navigating Disagreements

Disagreements are inevitable, but they can be resolved constructively:

4.5.1 Stay Calm: Keep emotions in check. Getting defensive or aggressive hampers productive dialogue.

4.5.2 Take Breaks: If a discussion becomes heated, it's okay to take a break and return to it later when emotions have settled.

4.5.3 Seek Compromise: Look for middle ground where both partners' concerns are addressed. Solutions often emerge through collaborative compromise.

4.6 Cultivating Regularity

Effective financial communication should be an ongoing practice:

4.6.1 Schedule Check-Ins: Regularly scheduled financial discussions prevent issues from festering and provide opportunities to recalibrate goals.

4.6.2 Celebrate Progress: Acknowledge achievements and progress in your financial journey. Celebrating milestones fosters a positive approach to financial communication.

4.6.3 Reflect and Adjust: After each conversation, partners should reflect on what went well and what could be improved. This self-awareness enhances future discussions.

4.7 Guided Conversation Exercises

To facilitate practical application, this chapter concludes with guided conversation exercises. These exercises encourage couples to engage in deliberate and focused financial discussions, fostering improved communication and understanding.

In the subsequent chapters, we'll explore methods for managing joint finances, aligning financial behaviors, and navigating financial challenges. By embracing effective communication techniques, couples can bridge the gap between divergent money perspectives, paving the way for a partnership rooted in shared understanding, empathy, and mutual growth.

5

Creating a Joint Budget

Financial stability within a partnership rests on the foundation of a well-structured budget. This chapter delves into the process of crafting a joint budget as a couple, guiding partners through the steps of tracking expenses, setting savings goals, and effectively managing debt.

5.1 The Importance of a Joint Budget

A joint budget serves as a roadmap for financial success, enabling partners to allocate resources, prioritize goals, and make informed decisions. This section underscores the role of a budget in establishing financial clarity and mutual accountability within a relationship.

5.2 The Budgeting Process

Crafting a joint budget involves a series of deliberate steps that foster collaboration and alignment:

5.2.1 Aggregate Income and Expenses: Compile both partners' sources of income and list all shared and individual expenses, categorizing them for clarity.

5.2.2 Set Shared Goals: Identify common financial goals, whether it's saving for a vacation, buying a home, or paying off debt. These shared aspirations provide a unifying purpose.

5.2.3 Allocate Funds: Allocate funds to different expense categories, considering both fixed and variable expenses. Partners should discuss and agree upon the distribution of funds.

5.2.4 Flexibility and Adjustments: A budget isn't static. Partners should be open to adjustments as circumstances change. Regularly revisit and modify the budget as needed.

5.3 Tracking Expenses

Accurate expense tracking is vital for staying on budget:

5.3.1 Digital Tools: Utilize budgeting apps and software that streamline the tracking process and provide real-time insights into spending patterns.

5.3.2 Regular Check-Ins: Set aside time each week or month to review spending. This helps identify areas where adjustments may be necessary.

5.3.3 Transparency: Transparently sharing expenses with each other fosters trust and enables partners to collectively manage their financial journey.

5.4 Saving Strategically

Savings are the foundation of financial security and achieving long-term goals:

5.4.1 Emergency Fund: Prioritize building an emergency fund to handle unforeseen expenses without derailing the budget.

5.4.2 Short-Term and Long-Term Goals: Allocate funds for both short-term goals (e.g., vacations) and long-term goals (e.g., retirement).

5.4.3 Automation: Automate contributions to savings accounts to ensure consistent progress towards goals.

5.5 Managing Debt

Debt management is a crucial aspect of financial well-being:

5.5.1 Debt Assessment: Assess and list all existing debts, including credit cards, loans, and other liabilities.

5.5.2 Debt Repayment Plan: Create a strategy for paying off debts efficiently, focusing on high-interest obligations first.

5.5.3 Open Communication: Discuss how to manage debt collectively, making joint decisions about prioritizing repayments.

5.6 Building in Flexibility

While budgets provide structure, they must also account for life's unpredictability:

5.6.1 Allow for Flexibility: Budgets should include a discretionary category for entertainment, leisure, and unexpected expenses.

5.6.2 Avoid Rigidity: A budget should not be so restrictive that it creates resentment. Balance is key.

5.6.3 Communication in Adjustments: When circumstances change, partners should communicate and collaboratively adjust the budget.

5.7 Guided Budgeting Exercises

To facilitate practical implementation, this chapter concludes with guided budgeting exercises. These exercises guide couples through the process of creating a budget, allocating funds, and setting financial goals.

In the subsequent chapters, we'll explore methods for addressing financial challenges, aligning financial behaviors, and securing a prosperous financial future. By crafting and adhering to a joint budget, couples can merge their financial aspirations, ensure transparency, and forge a path towards shared financial success.

6

Navigating Income Disparities

In today's diverse financial landscape, income disparities within partnerships are common. These disparities have the potential to affect dynamics if not managed thoughtfully. This chapter delves into the complexities of handling varying income levels and offers strategies for ensuring fairness, equity, and harmony in financial matters.

6.1 Embracing the Reality

Income disparities are a reality, often arising from career choices, educational backgrounds, or personal circumstances. Acknowledging these differences sets the stage for productive conversations:

6.1.1 Open Dialogue: Partners should openly discuss their respective incomes, addressing any discomfort or insecurities these discussions may bring up.

6.1.2 Shared Goals: While incomes may differ, shared financial goals can bring partners together, focusing on joint aspirations rather than the income divide.

6.1.3 Avoiding Assumptions: Income disparities don't define a person's financial attitudes. Partners should avoid assuming how the other person views money based solely on their income.

6.2 Approaching Financial Contributions

Partners must determine how to contribute to shared expenses and goals:

6.2.1 Proportional Contributions: Contributing a percentage of one's income ensures fairness. For example, if Partner A earns 60% of the combined income, they cover 60% of shared expenses.

6.2.2 Equitable Split: An equal division of expenses may be preferable if both partners value financial parity over proportional contributions.

6.2.3 Personal Accounts: Partners can maintain individual accounts for discretionary spending while contributing to a joint account for shared expenses.

6.3 Addressing Power Dynamics

Income disparities can sometimes lead to imbalances in decision-making:

6.3.1 Equal Voice: Regardless of income, each partner should have an equal say in financial decisions, ensuring that both perspectives are considered.

6.3.2 Open Discussions: Partners should actively discuss financial decisions, exploring how each person's input contributes to the overall well-being of the partnership.

6.3.3 Mutual Respect: Income differences should never undermine the respect partners have for each other. Both contributions, whether financial or otherwise, are valuable.

6.4 Avoiding Resentment

Income disparities can inadvertently lead to feelings of resentment if not managed effectively:

6.4.1 Expressing Appreciation: Regularly express gratitude for each other's contributions, whether financial or otherwise.

6.4.2 Celebrate Individual Successes: Celebrate each partner's achievements, reinforcing a supportive environment.

6.4.3 Addressing Feelings: If either partner feels undervalued due to income differences, addressing these feelings is crucial to prevent long-term resentment.

6.5 Joint Financial Goals

Shared financial aspirations can bridge the gap between income disparities:

6.5.1 Common Objectives: Focusing on joint goals, such as buying a house or funding education, creates a united front that surpasses individual incomes.

6.5.2 Combining Strengths: Partners can leverage their unique strengths—whether financial acumen, resourcefulness, or other attributes—to achieve shared goals.

6.5.3 Flexibility: Recognize that achieving certain goals may take longer due to income differences, and be open to adjusting timelines as needed.

6.6 Guided Conversation Exercises

To facilitate practical application, this chapter concludes with guided conversation exercises. These exercises encourage partners to explore their feelings about income disparities, discuss contribution strategies, and set joint financial goals.

In the subsequent chapters, we'll delve into overcoming financial challenges, aligning spending habits, and fostering financial intimacy. By navigating income disparities with empathy, respect, and a commitment to shared objectives, partners can forge a partnership that transcends financial differences and thrives on mutual understanding and growth.

7

Shared vs. Separate Finances

In the landscape of financial management within relationships, the debate between shared and separate finances is a common one. Each approach carries its own benefits and challenges. This chapter delves into the pros and cons of combining finances versus maintaining separate accounts, and also explores hybrid approaches that cater to various relationship dynamics.

7.1 Understanding the Spectrum

Financial management falls on a spectrum, with fully shared and completely separate finances at opposite ends. Partners should recognize that there's no one-size-fits-all solution:

7.1.1 Fully Shared Finances: In this approach, partners merge all accounts and manage finances jointly.

7.1.2 Separate Finances: In this approach, each partner maintains their own accounts and is responsible for their individual expenses.

7.1.3 Hybrid Approaches: Many couples find middle ground by combining certain aspects of their finances while maintaining some separation.

7.2 Pros and Cons of Shared Finances

Pros:

7.2.1 Transparency: Shared finances promote transparency, reducing the likelihood of hidden debts or financial secrets.

7.2.2 Simplicity: One combined account streamlines financial management and reduces administrative burden.

7.2.3 Teamwork: Joint finances encourage collaboration and a shared sense of financial responsibility.

Cons:

7.2.4 Decision Conflicts: Disagreements over spending priorities or financial decisions can lead to tension.

7.2.5 Loss of Autonomy: Individual autonomy in spending decisions may be limited.

7.2.6 Emotional Tensions: Shared finances can amplify emotional tensions if financial stress arises.

7.3 Pros and Cons of Separate Finances

Pros:

7.3.1 Autonomy: Each partner has full control over their own financial decisions.

7.3.2 Reduced Conflict: Separate finances can minimize disagreements about discretionary spending.

7.3.3 Financial Independence: Partners maintain individual financial independence and privacy.

Cons:

7.3.4 Communication Challenges: Separate finances can lead to a lack of transparency and difficulty in tracking joint financial goals.

7.3.5 Inequity: Income disparities can lead to feelings of inequity in financial contributions.

7.3.6 Missed Collaboration: Separate finances might hinder opportunities for collaborative decision-making.

7.4 Exploring Hybrid Approaches

7.4.1 Joint Expenses: Partners can maintain shared accounts for joint expenses, while also keeping individual accounts.

7.4.2 Personal Allowances: A hybrid approach could involve allocating individual spending allowances within a joint budget.

7.4.3 Clear Agreements: Hybrid approaches require clear agreements on what falls under shared responsibility and what is personal.

7.5 Choosing the Right Approach

The decision between shared and separate finances hinges on personal preferences, values, and goals:

7.5.1 Open Communication: Partners should engage in open conversations about their financial expectations and concerns.

7.5.2 Shared Goals: Aligning on shared goals can inform which financial approach best supports those objectives.

7.5.3 Flexibility: Recognize that financial approaches can evolve over time based on changing circumstances and preferences.

7.6 Guided Reflection and Discussion

To facilitate thoughtful consideration, this chapter concludes with guided reflection and discussion prompts. These prompts encourage partners to discuss their views on shared vs. separate finances and explore what approach aligns with their relationship dynamics.

In the forthcoming chapters, we'll explore strategies for addressing financial challenges, aligning financial behaviors, and cultivating financial intimacy. By consciously selecting an approach that resonates with their values and goals, couples can establish a financial framework that supports their shared journey and enhances their bond.

8

Saving for the Future

In the tapestry of financial well-being, saving for the future stands as a crucial thread. This chapter delves into the significance of setting aside funds for long-term goals and major expenses within a partnership. It also provides actionable tips for creating and maintaining a robust savings plan that supports a secure and fulfilling future.

8.1 The Importance of Long-Term Savings

Long-term savings form the foundation of financial security, ensuring a stable future:

8.1.1 Retirement: Planning for retirement is an essential component of long-term savings, allowing partners to maintain their quality of life in later years.

8.1.2 Major Expenses: Saving for major life events like buying a home, funding education, or starting a family requires careful financial preparation.

8.1.3 Financial Freedom: Long-term savings provide partners with a safety net, granting the freedom to pursue dreams and aspirations without undue financial stress.

8.2 Creating a Savings Plan

A structured savings plan empowers couples to proactively work towards their long-term goals:

8.2.1 Set Clear Goals: Clearly define your long-term goals, whether it's retiring comfortably or purchasing a home.

8.2.2 Calculate Required Savings: Determine how much you need to save for each goal and break it down into manageable milestones.

8.2.3 Prioritize and Allocate: Prioritize your goals and allocate funds accordingly. Some goals might require more immediate attention, while others can be long-term endeavors.

8.2.4 Automate Savings: Set up automated transfers to your savings accounts to ensure consistent contributions towards your goals.

8.3 Strategies for Maintaining a Savings Plan

Sustaining a savings plan requires discipline and adaptability:

8.3.1 Regular Check-Ins: Periodically review your savings plan to ensure you're on track and make adjustments if necessary.

8.3.2 Celebrate Milestones: Celebrate your progress towards your goals to stay motivated and reinforce positive financial behavior.

8.3.3 Emergency Fund: Maintain an emergency fund to cover unexpected expenses without derailing your long-term savings efforts.

8.3.4 Flexibility: Be flexible in your savings plan, especially when life circumstances change. Adapt your goals and contributions as needed.

8.4 Approaches for Joint Savings

Savings plans should align with your partnership's dynamics:

8.4.1 Shared Accounts: Utilize shared accounts for joint goals like buying a home or funding education.

8.4.2 Individual Accounts: Maintain individual savings accounts for personal goals, allowing partners to contribute according to their priorities.

8.4.3 Hybrid Approach: Combine shared and individual accounts to cater to both joint and personal goals.

8.5 Overcoming Challenges

Challenges may arise in maintaining a savings plan:

8.5.1 Income Fluctuations: Address income changes by adjusting your contributions while staying committed to your goals.

8.5.2 Lifestyle Inflation: Be cautious of lifestyle inflation that might hinder your savings efforts. Regularly revisit your budget to maintain a balance.

8.5.3 Unexpected Expenses: Be prepared for unexpected expenses that might temporarily affect your contributions.

8.6 Guided Planning Exercises

To facilitate practical application, this chapter concludes with guided planning exercises. These exercises assist couples in crafting their savings goals, creating a savings plan, and maintaining their commitment to a secure financial future.

In the upcoming chapters, we'll delve into strategies for overcoming financial challenges, aligning financial behaviors, and fostering financial intimacy. By nurturing a disciplined and adaptive approach to long-term savings, couples can lay the groundwork for a future that's financially sound and rich with possibilities.

9

Handling Debt Together

Debt can cast a shadow on financial well-being, but facing it together as a team can lead to transformative outcomes. This chapter delves into strategies for managing and reducing debt collaboratively within a partnership. It also explores the critical role of mutual support and accountability in overcoming financial challenges.

9.1 Acknowledging and Assessing Debt

The first step to overcoming debt is acknowledging its presence and understanding its scope:

9.1.1 Open Conversations: Partners should initiate candid conversations about their debts, sharing details about types, amounts, and interest rates.

9.1.2 Collaborative Assessment: Assess the overall impact of debt on your financial health, acknowledging how it affects your goals and aspirations.

9.1.3 Common Goals: Align on shared objectives for debt reduction, such as becoming debt-free or achieving a specific debt-to-income ratio.

9.2 Strategies for Debt Management

Handling debt effectively involves a combination of strategies and a united approach:

9.2.1 Consolidation: Consider consolidating multiple debts to simplify payments and potentially secure a lower interest rate.

9.2.2 Debt Payoff Plan: Collaboratively create a plan to pay off debts methodically. The debt snowball or avalanche methods can be effective approaches.

9.2.3 Budget Adjustments: Make necessary budget adjustments to allocate more funds towards debt repayment without sacrificing essentials.

9.2.4 Reduce Interest: Explore options to negotiate lower interest rates or refinance high-interest loans to ease the financial burden.

9.3 Role of Mutual Support

Navigating debt as a team requires unwavering mutual support:

9.3.1 Encouragement: Provide continuous encouragement and motivation to each other throughout the debt payoff journey.

9.3.2 Celebrate Wins: Celebrate milestones as you make progress in reducing debt, reinforcing positive financial behavior.

9.3.3 Emotional Support: Be a source of emotional support during challenging times, assuring each other that the journey is a shared endeavor.

9.4 Accountability Matters

Accountability is a cornerstone of successful debt management:

9.4.1 Regular Check-Ins: Schedule regular check-ins to track debt repayment progress, discuss challenges, and reassess your strategy if needed.

9.4.2 Joint Decision-Making: Collaboratively make financial decisions that affect debt reduction, fostering a sense of joint ownership.

9.4.3 Transparency: Maintain transparency about financial choices that might impact the debt repayment plan.

9.5 Overcoming Challenges

Debt repayment can be challenging, but facing these hurdles together is key:

9.5.1 Unexpected Expenses: Be prepared for unexpected financial emergencies that might temporarily divert resources from debt repayment.

9.5.2 Lifestyle Adjustments: Be willing to make temporary lifestyle adjustments to free up funds for debt reduction.

9.5.3 Patience: Debt repayment is a journey that requires patience. Celebrate progress while staying focused on the ultimate goal.

9.6 Guided Support Exercises

To facilitate practical application, this chapter concludes with guided support exercises. These exercises encourage couples to create a joint debt repayment plan, set mutual support goals, and establish accountability mechanisms.

In the forthcoming chapters, we'll delve into strategies for addressing financial challenges, aligning financial behaviors, and fostering financial intimacy. By approaching debt as a united front, partners can transform financial adversity into an opportunity for growth, solidarity, and a more secure future.

10

Investing and Financial Growth

Investing is the art of planting seeds today to reap a bountiful harvest tomorrow. This chapter delves into the world of investment options and strategies that can help couples build wealth and achieve their long-term financial goals. It also discusses how partners can collaboratively make informed investment decisions that align with their aspirations.

10.1 The Power of Investing

Investing is a critical component of wealth building and achieving financial goals:

10.1.1 Building Wealth: Investments offer the potential for significant financial growth over time, helping partners create a secure financial future.

10.1.2 Diversification: Investing across various assets minimizes risk and enhances the potential for higher returns.

10.1.3 Long-Term Focus: Investments thrive over the long term, making them ideal for partners with shared aspirations for the future.

10.2 Exploring Investment Options

Understanding different investment avenues is crucial for making informed decisions:

10.2.1 Stocks and Bonds: Stocks represent ownership in companies, while bonds are debt securities issued by corporations or governments.

10.2.2 Mutual Funds and ETFs: These are investment vehicles that pool money from multiple investors to invest in a diversified portfolio.

10.2.3 Real Estate: Investing in real estate, whether through property ownership or real estate investment trusts (REITs), offers potential appreciation and rental income.

10.2.4 Retirement Accounts: Contribute to retirement accounts like IRAs or 401(k)s to benefit from tax advantages while saving for the future.

10.3 Developing an Investment Strategy

Crafting a robust investment strategy requires thoughtful planning:

10.3.1 Define Goals: Clarify your financial goals, whether it's retirement, buying a home, or funding education.

10.3.2 Risk Tolerance: Assess your risk tolerance and investment timeline, aligning your strategy with your comfort level.

10.3.3 Asset Allocation: Diversify your portfolio across different asset classes to manage risk and optimize returns.

10.3.4 Regular Contributions: Make regular contributions to your investments, benefiting from the power of compounding.

10.4 Collaborative Decision-Making

Making investment decisions as a team is crucial for mutual alignment:

10.4.1 Shared Vision: Ensure that your investment choices align with your shared financial goals and values.

10.4.2 Research Together: Collaboratively research investment options, staying informed about potential risks and rewards.

10.4.3 Seek Professional Advice: Consult financial advisors to gain expert insights and recommendations based on your unique circumstances.

10.5 Managing Investments Together

Ongoing management is key to successful investing:

10.5.1 Regular Review: Periodically review your investment portfolio to assess performance and make necessary adjustments.

10.5.2 Stay Informed: Keep up with economic trends, market conditions, and changes that might impact your investments.

10.5.3 Long-Term Perspective: Investing is a marathon, not a sprint. Maintain a patient and long-term perspective.

10.6 Overcoming Challenges

Investing comes with its challenges, but they can be addressed together:

10.6.1 Market Volatility: Be prepared for market fluctuations and avoid making impulsive decisions based on short-term trends.

10.6.2 Communication: Regularly communicate about your investment decisions, ensuring you're both on the same page.

10.6.3 Adjustments: Be open to adjusting your investment strategy as your goals, risk tolerance, and circumstances change.

10.7 Guided Investment Exercises

To facilitate practical application, this chapter concludes with guided investment exercises. These exercises encourage couples to set investment goals, research investment options, and create a joint investment strategy.

In the subsequent chapters, we'll explore strategies for addressing financial challenges, aligning financial behaviors, and fostering financial intimacy. By venturing into the world of investing as a united front, couples can harness the power of financial growth and lay the groundwork for a prosperous future.

11

Handling Financial Challenges

Life is filled with uncertainties, and financial challenges are an inevitable part of the journey. This chapter delves into strategies for addressing unexpected financial hurdles as a team within a partnership. It offers guidance on navigating these challenges while preserving the strength and harmony of the relationship.

11.1 Embracing the Unpredictable

Financial challenges can strike unexpectedly, but a united approach can make them more manageable:

11.1.1 Shared Perspective: Understand that financial challenges are external to the relationship and don't define your partnership.

11.1.2 Preparedness: Create an emergency fund to provide a safety net during unexpected financial downturns.

11.1.3 Team Mindset: Approach challenges as a united team, pooling resources and strengths to overcome them.

11.2 Navigating Emergencies

Addressing emergencies requires a combination of practicality and emotional support:

11.2.1 Assess the Situation: Evaluate the nature and scope of the emergency, determining the immediate and long-term impact.

11.2.2 Prioritize Expenses: Focus on essential expenses like housing, food, and utilities while cutting back on discretionary spending.

11.2.3 Seek Help: If the situation is dire, consider seeking financial advice, government assistance, or community support.

11.3 Coping with Job Loss

Job loss can be emotionally challenging, but navigating it together can lessen the burden:

11.3.1 Supportive Environment: Create an environment where partners can openly discuss fears, concerns, and potential solutions.

11.3.2 Financial Evaluation: Reassess your budget and prioritize spending to accommodate the new financial situation.

11.3.3 Job Search Collaboration: Collaborate on job searching efforts, leveraging each other's networks and skills.

11.4 Preserving Relationship Harmony

Financial challenges can strain a relationship, but taking a proactive approach can help maintain harmony:

11.4.1 Open Communication: Keep lines of communication open, sharing feelings, concerns, and strategies for managing the challenge.

11.4.2 Problem-Solving Together: Collaboratively brainstorm solutions, tapping into each other's creativity and resourcefulness.

11.4.3 Blame-Free Zone: Avoid blaming each other for the situation. Focus on finding solutions rather than assigning fault.

11.5 Leveraging Strengths

Partners can use their unique strengths to tackle challenges:

11.5.1 Financial Expertise: If one partner has more financial knowledge, they can guide the partnership's financial decisions.

11.5.2 Emotional Support: Offer emotional support and encouragement, demonstrating your commitment to facing challenges together.

11.5.3 Resourcefulness: Both partners can leverage their skills to find creative solutions and opportunities.

11.6 Guided Resilience Exercises

To facilitate practical application, this chapter concludes with guided resilience exercises. These exercises encourage couples to explore their support strategies, discuss emergency plans, and strengthen their ability to face challenges together.

In the upcoming chapters, we'll delve into strategies for aligning financial behaviors, fostering financial intimacy, and building a resilient financial foundation. By navigating financial challenges with empathy, collaboration, and a shared sense of purpose, couples can transform adversity into an opportunity for growth and strength in their partnership.

12

The Power of Financial Partnership

As you've embarked on the journey of managing money as a team, it's important to reflect on the lessons learned, the growth achieved, and the potential for a brighter financial future. This chapter encapsulates the essence of your journey, summarizes key takeaways, and provides guidance for sustaining a healthy and harmonious financial partnership.

12.1 Reflecting on the Journey

Reflecting on your financial partnership journey can offer insights into your growth as individuals and as a couple:

12.1.1 Shared Accomplishments: Celebrate the milestones you've achieved together, whether it's paying off debt, reaching savings goals, or making informed investment decisions.

12.1.2 Learning Experiences: Embrace the challenges you've faced as opportunities for growth and learning, fostering resilience and adaptability.

12.1.3 Emotional Connection: Recognize how open communication and collaboration in financial matters have strengthened your emotional bond.

12.2 Key Takeaways

Your journey has provided valuable lessons that can shape your ongoing financial partnership:

12.2.1 Communication Is Key: Open, honest, and respectful communication is the cornerstone of a healthy financial partnership.

12.2.2 Shared Goals Matter: Aligning on shared financial goals drives your collective efforts and strengthens your sense of purpose.

12.2.3 Financial Transparency: Transparency in sharing financial information fosters trust, transparency, and accountability.

12.2.4 Mutual Support: Supporting each other emotionally and practically during financial challenges deepens your partnership.

12.3 Sustaining a Healthy Financial Partnership

As you move forward, consider these strategies for maintaining a strong financial partnership:

12.3.1 Regular Check-Ins: Schedule regular discussions to review your financial goals, assess progress, and make adjustments as needed.

12.3.2 Evolve Together: Recognize that your financial situation and goals may change over time. Adapt your strategies accordingly.

12.3.3 Continuous Learning: Stay informed about financial matters through ongoing learning and seeking advice when needed.

12.3.4 Flexibility: Embrace flexibility in your approach to finances, knowing that life's circumstances are dynamic.

12.4 Nurturing Financial Intimacy

As you deepen your financial partnership, consider these steps to enhance financial intimacy:

12.4.1 Shared Financial Dreams: Discuss and visualize your long-term financial dreams and aspirations together.

12.4.2 Collaborative Decision-Making: Involve each other in major financial decisions, ensuring both perspectives are valued.

12.4.3 Mutual Growth: Approach your financial journey as an opportunity for mutual growth, supporting each other's development.

12.5 Guided Reflection and Forward Vision

To facilitate reflection and forward planning, this chapter concludes with guided reflection exercises. These exercises encourage couples to reflect on their financial journey, define their vision for the future, and set intentions for maintaining a strong financial partnership.

As you step into the future, remember that your financial partnership is a dynamic and evolving aspect of your relationship. By embracing the power of collaboration, communication, and mutual support, you can navigate financial challenges and opportunities as a united team, strengthening the foundation of your partnership and fostering a prosperous and harmonious life together.

Absolutely, here's a detailed Conclusion for your book, emphasizing the significance of teamwork in managing relationship finances and encouraging readers to approach financial matters with transparency, communication, and shared goals:

Conclusion: Navigating Financial Waters Together

Congratulations! You've embarked on a journey that's not only about money but about the strength of your partnership. Managing finances as a team is a profound testament to the depth of your commitment to each other. Throughout this book, you've explored the intricacies of financial management within a relationship and gained insights into how to navigate the complexities of money matters.

The Power of Teamwork

At the heart of successful financial partnership lies the power of teamwork. Just as a ship navigates rough waters more effectively with a capable crew, your relationship benefits immensely from the combined efforts, insights, and perspectives that both of you bring to the table. You've learned that aligning your financial goals, communicating openly, and facing challenges together can lead to financial harmony and emotional closeness.

Transparency and Communication: The Bedrock

Transparency and communication have been recurring themes throughout this journey. By openly sharing your financial dreams, fears, and realities, you've built a foundation of trust that bolsters your financial partnership. The conversations you've had about money have deepened your understanding of each other and fostered a sense of unity. These conversations may not always be easy, but they are crucial for creating a solid financial framework.

Shared Goals: The North Star

Shared goals are the North Star guiding your financial journey. When you unite behind common aspirations—whether it's owning a home, retiring comfortably, or simply leading a fulfilling life—you set yourselves on a trajectory that strengthens your resolve to overcome challenges. Shared goals infuse purpose into your financial decisions and remind you that you're working towards something greater than money itself.

Fostering a Prosperous Future

As you move forward, remember that managing finances isn't just about dollars and cents; it's about nurturing your relationship's growth and prosperity. Approach financial matters with the same care, consideration, and love you bring to other aspects of your partnership. Whether you're celebrating achievements, facing setbacks, or making decisions, remember that you're in this together.

Embrace the Journey

Your journey doesn't end here—it's an ongoing adventure that will continue to evolve as your lives and circumstances change. Embrace the highs and navigate the lows with the same dedication and teamwork that you've shown thus far. By maintaining transparency, open communication, and a shared vision, you'll foster a dynamic financial partnership that thrives on your mutual respect and shared commitment.

Here's to Your Financial Success!

May your financial journey be marked by growth, resilience, and shared achievements. As you build your future together, carry the lessons you've learned and the principles you've embraced—transparency, communication, shared goals, and teamwork—with you. With these tools in hand, you're well-equipped to overcome any financial challenge and create a prosperous, harmonious life together.

Cheers to your financial success and to the enduring strength of your partnership!

49